Hope for the Broken Spirit

Hope for the Broken Spirit

Poetry and Scriptures to Heal the Wounds of
Depression and Hopelessness

Glenn Goree

RESOURCE *Publications* • Eugene, Oregon

HOPE FOR THE BROKEN SPIRIT
Poetry and Scriptures to Heal the Wounds of Depression and Hopelessness

Copyright © 2016 Glenn Goree. All rights reserved. Except for brief quotations in critical publications or reviews, no part of this book may be reproduced in any manner without prior written permission from the publisher. Write: Permissions, Wipf and Stock Publishers, 199 W. 8th Ave., Suite 3, Eugene, OR 97401.

Resource Publications
An Imprint of Wipf and Stock Publishers
199 W. 8th Ave., Suite 3
Eugene, OR 97401

www.wipfandstock.com

PAPERBACK ISBN: 978-1-5326-0673-1
HARDCOVER ISBN: 978-1-5326-0675-5
EBOOK ISBN: 978-1-5326-0674-8

Manufactured in the U.S.A.   SEPTEMBER 15, 2016

Scripture is taken from the Holy Bible, New International Version, NIV. Copyright 1973, 1978, 1984 by International Bible Society. Used by permission of Zondervan. All rights reserved worldwide.

I dedicate these poems to all the clients I counseled over the last thirty years who suffered from depression and anxiety.

Contents

Introduction | ix

Day One	The Art of Hope	1
Day Two	The Security of Our Father's Hope	2
Day Three	Last or First Hope	3
Day Four	Our Master's Final Walk	4
Day Five	Hope, a Promise We Can Savor	5
Day Six	Hope, the Answer to Depression	6
Day Seven	Hope Bears the Cost	8
Day Eight	Hope that Withstands the Human Tempest	9
Day Nine	Hope of a Higher Altitude	10
Day Ten	The Hope of the Great *I AM*	11
Day Eleven	Hope Never Gives Up	12
Day Twelve	Hope Turns Not Away	13
Day Thirteen	How God Moves	14
Day Fourteen	Innocent Hope	15
Day Fifteen	Hope, Food for the Soul	16
Day Sixteen	Hope of a Doting Father	17
Day Seventeen	Hope, Genuine and Eternal	18
Day Eighteen	Hope, Waiting to be Claimed	19
Day Nineteen	The Struggle to Believe in Hope	20
Day Twenty	Soar with Hope	21
Day Twenty-One	Hope for the Sightless	22
Day Twenty-Two	Hope of the Nazarene	23

Contents

Day Twenty-Three	Hope of Hidden Worth | 24
Day Twenty-Four	Hope of the Snowflake | 25
Day Twenty-Five	Unseen Hope | 26
Day Twenty-Six	Hope over Satan | 27
Day Twenty-Seven	Hope for the Doubting Thomas | 28
Day Twenty-Eight	Hope, the Source of Strength | 29
Day Twenty-Nine	Hope When There's None | 30
Day Thirty	Hope's Afterglow | 31
Day Thirty-One	Hope's Eternal Land | 32
Day Thirty-Two	Intangible Hope | 33
Day Thirty-Three	Stay the Course | 34
Day Thirty-Four	Hope Leads Home | 35
Day Thirty-Five	Perfect Love in Hope | 36
Day Thirty-Six	Simplicity of Hope | 37

Conclusion | 38

Introduction

> "How long, O Lord? Will you forget me forever? How long will you hide your face from me? How long must I wrestle with my thoughts and every day have sorrow in my heart?"
>
> (PSALM 13:1–2)

WHAT COMES FIRST, DEPRESSION or hopelessness? I've asked myself that question for over thirty years. In my practice as a counselor most of my cases, in one form or another, involve both hopelessness and depression. At first, I thought their hopelessness was a symptom of depression. However, in time and with experience, I began to ask, "Did my client give up hope in life and then become depressed? Or, did my client become depressed, and then after a while, feel hopeless because of depression?"

I've come to believe that hopelessness comes first, resulting in depression. Consider a true life example. A young man completes his college education, graduating with honors. The new scholar filled with excitement and enthusiasm hits the streets looking for a job. A month goes by, then two. Before the excited young person realizes it, a year has come and gone and he still has no job. The student has salt poured in his academic wounds when he learns several friends who graduated with lower grades have secured jobs, and have been working and earning money.

As an automobile tire flattens because of a puncture, so too does our young college grad feel deflated by hopelessness because life has punctured his expectations. Depression follows, and soon he contacts someone like me for counseling.

It is my desire that this book of poems will act as an infusion of air to inflate the new tire of hope.

The key to a resolving any issue in counseling is consistency. With this thought in mind I have prepared thirty-six poems along with scriptures from God's Word. My suggested goal is to set aside a few quiet moments

Introduction

each day. Use this time to read one poem and accompanying scripture, and in solitude, offer a prayer to God.

It is my prayer that as you follow these devotionals they will be part of a spiritual awakening in the hope you have in Jesus.

Day One
The Art of Hope

I love you Lord with all my heart.
In you alone I find my daily start.
Hope in you, I find is an art.
Please teach me Lord, to know my part.

"The Lord is close to the broken hearted and saves those who are crushed in spirit. A righteous man may have many troubles, but the Lord delivers him from them all; he protects all his bones, not one of them will be broken."

(PSALM 34:18-20)

Day Two
The Security of Our Father's Hope

There, standing at the window, then in the street,
A worried father searches for his son to greet.

How many times has the father followed this vigilance?
How many times has he thought he saw his son at a glance?

Strained eyes, broken heart, downcast face,
Again the father turns to his house without a trace.

Is this not how our Father in heaven feels?
He doesn't believe His offer of hope is on spinning wheels.

Our Father's promise is more secure than a bank loan,
Because His Son's death secured it with nary a groan.

"You do not delight in sacrifice, or I would bring it; you do not take pleasure in burnt offerings. The sacrifices of God are a broken spirit; a broken and contrite heart, O God, you will not despise."

(PSALM 51:16–17)

Day Three
Last or First Hope

Last hope or first hope,
Where is Christ in our spiritual scope?

Sometimes we say the latter over the former,
Until burdens cause us to be spiritual reformers.

"Praise the Lord. How good it is to sing praises to our God, how pleasant and fitting to praise him! The Lord builds up Jerusalem; he gathers the exiles of Israel. He heals the broken hearted and binds up their wounds."

(PSALM 147:1–3)

Day Four
Our Master's Final Walk

A podiatrist's dream comes true,
My trotters ache from walking miles in shoes with threads showing through.

Have they not trudged on swampy land and riverbank late at night?
Has their owner not compelled them on, in spite of mortal fright?

Worn dogs they were after traversing remote African bush trails,
Calluses, blisters, and sores have scarred their flesh and toenails.

And sports—don't forget exhaustion's temperance
Bringing youth's exuberance to its painful remembrance.

Yet, never have they embraced our Master's final walk,
Bearing a wooden beam, empty lungs so he could not talk.

Then, nailed to a cross with iron piercing ankle, sinew, and bone,
All because He gave us hope to never face our sin alone.

"I will exalt you, O Lord, for you lifted me out of the depths and did not let my enemies gloat over me. O Lord my God, I called to you for help and you healed me. O Lord, you brought me up from the grave; you spared me from going down into the pit."

(PSALM 30:1–3)

Day Five
Hope, a Promise We Can Savor

Why do we say no?
He's there, in rain, sleet, or snow.

When do we say yes?
When it's His will we try to guess.

Do you suppose we should be content?
That we accept whatever is sent?

Because His will is for our best,
No matter what life's test.

This is why God gave us hope through our Savior,
For in His Son we find promise we can savor.

"The Lord is my light and my salvation—whom shall I fear? The Lord is the stronghold of my life—of whom shall I be afraid? When evil men advance against me to devour my flesh, when my enemies and my foes attack me, they will stumble and fall. Though an army besiege me, my heart will not fear; though war break out against me, even then will I be confident."

(PSALM 27:1–3)

Day Six
Hope, the Answer to Depression

Hope is a state of a love that believes in a God above.

Depression is what takes it away,
Robbing joy and life, day after day.

Slithering and sidewinding, it makes its way,
Seeking a home in which it can stay.

Look up not down, at your slightest frown.

Raise your hands high, and point to the sky.

Lift your face toward Jehovah's life giving sun,
Feel its reviving warmth as though embracing God's Son.

Realize hope is what Satan seeks to take,
Because he doesn't love God's pearly gate.

If you allow him to enter your mortal flesh and bone,
If you let him, he can make you feel lost and alone.

Sometimes we must shout, "Enough! Get away from me,
Because I belong to the Marker of earth, sky and sea.

Be gone, you Serpent of the air, into your eyes I will no longer stare."

Then reach with soul's eternal might, to embrace the One who won your fight.

"I sought the Lord, and he answered me; he delivered me from all my fears. Those who look to him are radiant; their faces are never covered with shame. This poor man called, and the Lord heard him; he saved him out of all his troubles. The angel of the Lord encamps around those who fear him, and he delivers them."

(PSALM 34:4–7)

Day Seven
Hope Bears the Cost

All is lost. I can't bear the cost.

Valiant in my effort to the end
Of life and treasure, all lost to the wind.

Can I expect a tomorrow's morn?
Where I can mend a life so torn?

All seems to fade to darkness, hence I cannot see,
Except for doom's dark shadow hanging over me.

That is why God's Son hung on a tree,
Because in His death he offered what mortals cannot see.

His eyes share hope of another kind,
Where sin can our souls no longer bind.

"The Lord delights in the way of the man whose steps he has made firm; though he stumble, he will not fall, for the Lord upholds him with his hand."

(PSALM 37:23-24)

Day Eight
Hope that Withstands the Human Tempest

Are we in this world because of an undisciplined randomness?
No. We will one day answer to God, in all candidness.

For God preordained His Son to fulfill a special circumstance—
Heaven's unique plan of eternal romance,
Where He died for His bride, to foil Satan's darkest dance,
Offering all who call on His name a second chance.

How, then, can anyone question our hope found in His life?
Did He not die to end our mortal toil and unholy strife?
He as good as held to His own throat the Reaper's knife.

Therefore, let us never forget when we are at our weakest,
The sacrifice Jesus made for us when we feel our cheapest.
For we live in hope that withstands our human tempest.

"Praise the Lord. Blessed is the man who fears the Lord, who finds great delight in his commands. He will have no fear of bad news; his heart is steadfast, trusting in the Lord. His heart is secure, he will have no fear; in the end he will look in triumph on his foes."

(PSALM 112:1, 7–8)

Day Nine
Hope of a Higher Altitude

Dictators, presidents, kings, and queens,
Governments are full of these earthly beings.

All promise hope and change,
But neither is within their range.

Because humans are not God,
Since on this imperfect world they trod.

Hope and change are found on knees,
Pray morning, noon, and night. He hears our pleas.

In the dark we lay flat on the floor,
Pouring out our hearts due to weaknesses we deplore.

And in this honest, humbling attitude,
We will discover a hope of a higher altitude.

"Your word is a lamp to my feet and a light for my path. I have taken an oath and confirmed it, then I will follow your righteous laws."

(PSALM 119:105-106)

Day Ten
The Hope of the Great *I AM*

What is this test?
I gave my all, my best,
Still, it's insufficient. Therefore, I make a humble request

To the God of Abraham
Who defeated Satan's sham.
For it was in blood, not of goat or ram,
That my hope is found in the great *I AM*.

"I will lie down and sleep in peace, for you alone, O Lord, make me dwell in safety."

(PSALM 4:8)

Day Eleven
Hope Never Gives Up

I think what exacerbates
The frustration when seeking the pearly gates,
Is seeing those who don't care one way or other,
Seemingly glide through life with nary a bother.

Maybe 'tis better to give in and not be concerned with sin.

For what use is a life reaching for holiness
When in fact, it is filled with hopelessness?

This helpless feeling in mind requires an attitude of a different kind,

One like Jesus demonstrated over this selfsame defeat.
But instead, chose to confront and permanently unseat

His adversary, the devil, by His death on the cross of pain.
So that those who call Him brother could wear His name,

And one day be found among His faithful few,
Who, in His promise, did what they were supposed to.

"Give ear to my words, O Lord, consider my sighing. Listen to my cry for help, my King and my God for to you I pray. Morning by morning, O Lord, you hear my voice; morning by morning I lay my requests before you and wait in expectation."

(PSALM 5:1–3)

Day Twelve
Hope Turns Not Away

Hey, don't turn your face away.
Don't you want to hear what I have to say?

How often does God say this to us?
Was His Son not nailed to a board and truss?

What if God turned away his face?
We'd have no hope to escape our mortal place.

But God never treats us as we treat Him.
This is why we praise Him with word and hymn.

"I am worn out from groaning; all night long I flood my bed with weeping and drench my couch with tears. My eyes grow weak with sorrow; they fail because of all my foes. Away from me, all you who do evil, for the Lord has heard my weeping. The Lord has heard my cry for mercy; the Lord accepts my prayer."

(PSALM 6:6–9)

Day Thirteen
How God Moves

How does God walk?
Without legs, does He sometime balk?

After all, in less than a blink of an eye,
He's everywhere because He's an omnipresent guy.

Then why do we read of His walk, steps, and path?
Seems to me these terms don't add up even with special math.

I think it's because His other two Omni's offer our only hope,
So He lets us know in mortal terms, understandable,
He is always there with His promise not remittable.

"The Lord is a refuge for the oppressed, a stronghold in times of trouble. Those who know your name will trust in you, for you, Lord, have never forsaken those who seek you."

(PSALM 9:9-10)

Day Fourteen
Innocent Hope

A heart tender and sweet,
'Tis juicy from Satan's conceit.

A heart young in innocence,
Satan offers a deceptive fragrance.

Is there hope for rescue eternal?
Or shall most be in Satan's journal?

Yes. That forever rest,
Was purchased by God's best.

His Son's blood covers,
The sins of His redeemed lovers.

"Look on me and answer, O Lord my God. Give light to my eyes, or I will sleep in death; my enemy will say, 'I have overcome him,' and my foes will rejoice when I fall. But I trust in your unfailing love; my heart rejoices in your salvation. I will sing to the Lord, for he has been good to me."

(PSALM 13:3-6)

Day Fifteen
Hope, Food for the Soul

What in life is needed most?
For what do we appeal through our Holy Ghost?

Is not hope our greatest sustenance,
Something we pray for in abundance?

Hope's diet dare not be rationed,
For then its promise forfeits its passion.

God is hope's sole source.
Without Him there is a spiritual divorce.

So let us sup at His Son's table
With a feast of bread and wine to make us stable.

For in his love alone
We will discover a heavenly home.

"Keep me safe, O God, for in you I take refuge. I said to the Lord,
'You are my Lord; apart from you I have no good thing.'"

(PSALM 16:1-2)

Day Sixteen
Hope of a Doting Father

Do you think God sometimes sits up concerned late at night,
Worrying like a doting father about our mortal spiritual fight?

When he looks down from his safe home in heaven above,
Would he gather us like a hen protecting her young with wings of love?

This gift we call hope through His son passionately revealed,
Was it not purchased in his blood on sin's battle field?

Then let us, one and all, of a common family and kin,
Tenaciously grasp its promise that allows us to live again.

"The Lord is my shepherd, I shall lack nothing. He makes me lie down in green pastures, he leads me beside quiet waters, he restores my soul. He guides me in paths of righteousness for his name's sake. Even though I walk through the valley of the shadow of death, I will fear no evil, for you are with me; your rod and your staff, they comfort me. You prepare a table before me in the presence of my enemies. You anoint my head with oil; my cup overflows. Surely goodness and love will follow me all the days of my life, and I will dwell in the house of the Lord forever."

(PSALM 23)

Day Seventeen
Hope, Genuine and Eternal

Mercy seat—
It cleanses all at its feet.

How else could we defeat
Satan in his self-conceit?

Because he believes through his deceit,
That on *the* day he will cheat

Our God of his children to whom he offers hope,
That is beyond their mortal grasp and scope,

Of a promise to all who offer,
Their souls to God and not to Satan's coffer.

And these faithful few will be with their loving Father,
Who will give their souls rest so they won't need to search any further.

"One thing I ask of the Lord, this is what I seek: that I may dwell in the house of the Lord all the days of my life, to gaze upon the beauty of the Lord and to seek him in his temple."

(PSALM 27:4)

Day Eighteen
Hope, Waiting to be Claimed

It's never too late.
So please don't hesitate
To make a unique and special date
For your soul's hope of an eternal state.

Your name is written on the pearly gate,
Waiting at the end of your speedy gait
To claim your new mansion and estate.

"I am still confident of this: I will see the goodness of the Lord in the land of the living. Wait for the Lord; be strong and take heart and wait for the Lord."

(PSALM 27:13-14)

Day Nineteen
The Struggle to Believe in Hope

Clashing swords. See the sparks fly?
Watch as two foes seek to make the other die.

Shields at the ready to block each blow,
Without their protection, the combatants would be brought low.

One will die, and the other will live.
A spirit lost in youth, never more to give.

But look and examine closer the determined two contestants.
No! There's but one soul, with divided loyalties, insistent.

"There's no hope!" yells one. "You fool. What's promised is only a dream."
While the other knows love is wrapped in a veil with no seam.

Is this not the struggle each of us fights?
One day believing and the next we run from Satan in fright.

Hang on to the Cross with all your heart's might,
And Jesus will hold on to you who are always in His sight.

"But I trust in you, O Lord; I say, 'You are my God.' My times are in your hand; deliver me from my enemies and from those who pursue me. Let your face shine on your servant; save me in your unfailing love. Let me not be put to shame, O Lord, for I have cried out to you; but let the wicked be put to shame and lie silent in the grave. Let their lying lips be silenced, for with pride and contempt they speak arrogantly against the righteous."

(PSALM 31:14–18)

Day Twenty
Soar with Hope

I want to soar above this mortal floor,
Beyond flesh short-lived, keeping score,
No longer entangled midst life's fruitless chore.

How, pray tell, is this accomplished, I implore?

Listen closely for the salve to heal sin's sore
Is hope, God's answer for those he adores.

"But the eyes of the Lord are on those who fear him, on those whose hope is in his unfailing love, to deliver them from death and keep them alive in famine. We wait in hope for the Lord; he is our help and our shield. In him our hearts rejoice, for we trust in his holy name. May your unfailing love rest upon us, O Lord, even as we put our hope in you."

(PSALM 33:18-22)

Day Twenty-One
Hope for the Sightless

All is lost. I can't bear the cost.

Valiant in my effort to the end
Of life and treasure, all lost to the wind.

Can I expect tomorrow's morn
Where I can mend a life so torn?

All seems to fade to darkness, hence I cannot see,
Except for doom's dark shadow hanging over me.

This is why our God's Son hung on a tree,
Because in His death He offers what mortals can't see.

His eyes share hope of another kind,
Where sin can our souls no longer bind.

"Evil will slay the wicked; the foes of the righteous will be condemned. The Lord redeems his servants; no one who takes refuge in him will be condemned."

(PSALM 34:21–22)

Day Twenty-Two
Hope of the Nazarene

Today is another day.
Shouldn't throw it all away,
Just because I made a slip yesterday.

Are we not all sinners in one way or another?
Have we not all blown our spiritual cover?

It's at this time we seek a holy other,
One who gives hope because He's our brother?

This Jesus, whom many doubt and disparage,
Gives us a promise delivered from a celestial carriage,
Because His bride, the church, with Him has a holy marriage,

So when you feel down for the count of ten,
Remember whom you believed in,
As this Nazarene of Judah is our next of kin,
He offers hope of life to begin again,
And a promise given, no matter the sin.

"The Lord delights in the way of the man whose steps he has made firm; though he stumble, he will not fall, for the Lord upholds him with his hand."

(PSALM 37:23–24)

Day Twenty-Three
Hope of Hidden Worth

Pain sought after,
Hanging by nails from life's rafter.
Why do we not prefer truth over laughter?

At the time, all seems happy and carefree,
Not facing what we know hidden to be.
There's a concealed price that will lower us to the knee,
Allowing us to choose a master we'll serve eternally.

Therefore, select now the hope you know is a guarantee.

Be not fooled by Satan's appeals to the flesh,
Whose promises intertwine souls with his mesh.

Bow to the Lord of heaven and earth,
Who was offered gold, frankincense, and myrrh,
Because He alone gives hope by His blood of eternal worth.

"I waited patiently for the Lord; he turned to me and heard my cry. He lifted me out of the slimy pit, out of the mud and mire; he set my feet on a rock and gave me a firm place to stand. He put a new song in my mouth, a hymn of praise to our God. Many will see and fear and put their trust in the Lord."

(PSALM 40:1–3)

Day Twenty-Four
Hope of the Snowflake

Oh, the delicacy of a snowflake!
Who but God can one so easily make?

Intricate beyond compare,
Falling from the heavens for all to share.

So if in less than the blink of an eye
God creates this wonder, causing a sigh,

Is it any less a miracle He gave His Son to die
So believers would have more than a grave in which to lie?

No. Because his vision from the beginning of man
Has been to provide an eternal plan.

That no matter how much pain in life they suffer,
He has given this hope as an eternal buffer.

"God is our refuge and strength, an ever present help in trouble. Therefore we will not fear, though the earth give way and the mountains fall into the heart of the sea, though its waters roar and foam and the mountains quake with their surging."

(PSALM 46:1–3)

Day Twenty-Five
Unseen Hope

Pass it and run.
Does this mean we are done?

No. I am in great haste,
Fearful of time's waste.

"Slow down," I plead,
"Something else you need."

Be not consumed with the here and now,
Rather think beyond the labor of earth's horse and plow.

Toil for mortal life is only temporary,
But to prepare for eternity should be primary.

Therefore, invest in the Savior's hope of what is unseen,
And receive the Lamb's promise of being eternally clean.

"Cast your cares on the Lord and he will sustain you; he will never let the righteous fall."

(PSALM 55:22)

Day Twenty-Six
Hope over Satan

Death's hold to which humans migrate,
What for mortals doth liberate?

Works, deeds, virtue's renewing?
Please inform of death's undoing.

Hope found in Christ's sacrifice,
This promise alone doth suffice.

"Have mercy on me, O God, have mercy on me, for in you my soul takes refuge. I will take refuge in the shadow of your wings until the disaster has passed."

(PSALM 57:1)

Day Twenty-Seven
Hope for the Doubting Thomas

How are you doing?
I'm fine, because I'm still moving.

Is there a chance for improving?
Not today, because over yesterday I'm still stewing.

Is this dialogue not reflecting
A hope in Christ we are misconnecting?

Everyday should be a great day in the Nazarene,
No matter who or what has treated us mean.

"Why?" you might ask in bewilderment,
Life as we know it is no sweet testament.

You have made my proposition's point
Because with His love daily He does anoint

Every one of His followers with a sound promise,
That was confirmed two thousand years ago by doubting Thomas.

"Hear my cry, O God; listen to my prayer. From the ends of the earth I call to you, I call as my heart grows faint; lead me to the rock that is higher than I."

(PSALM 61:1–2)

Day Twenty-Eight
Hope, the Source of Strength

Onward we go,
Facing the foe,
Sometimes fast, sometimes slow.

But forward we tread,
Facing the enemy ahead,
Sometimes with bravery, sometimes with dread.

Pray tell, what gives us the strength?
Is it what lies ahead, above, or beneath?
In what power do we discover our zenith?

The answer is in the only One who offers hope,
Whose promise is as solid as rock, and above mortal scope,
And is sealed by His blood from a cross of wood, nails, and rope.

"Find rest, O my soul, in God alone; my hope comes from him. He alone is my rock and my salvation; he is my fortress, I will not be shaken. My salvation and my honor depend on God; he is my mighty rock, my refuge. Trust in him at all times, O people; pour out your hearts to him, for God is our refuge."

(PSALM 62:5–8)

Day Twenty-Nine
Hope When There's None

Beneath a tree lays a restful, green bed,
For a soul who no longer on earth does tread.

His life was given for his loving family,
In his travels over land, air, and sea.

At times he felt he could give no more.
All was lost, so nothing could even his score.

God reminded him in hope he was never alone,
That he had a God who cared for his every bone.

He then lifted up his soul to higher engage,
In a greater pursuit beyond this age.

"My flesh and my heart may fail, but God is the strength of my heart and my portion forever."

(PSALM 73:26)

Day Thirty
Hope's Afterglow

Oh abjured eye,
Cast not your tainted gaze to the sky,
And feel death's embrace when you die.

All is not lost until breath's final sigh.

Repent, and turn to your only hope,
Escape Satan's noose and hangman's rope,
Recede not to a lesser eternal scope.

For there's a Savior high and low,
Willing to love when told no.
He offers a promise in humility's glow.
Therefore, give Him your life so you will know,
Forgiveness's sweet afterglow.

"How lovely is your dwelling place, O Lord almighty! My soul yearns, even faints for the courts of the Lord; my heart and my flesh cry out for the living God."

(PSALM 84:1-2)

Day Thirty-One
Hope's Eternal Land

What mortal mind
Found intertwined
With flesh's covert bind,
Doesn't feel undermined?

What sets us free
Upon bended knee?

When we come to God in humility
He then helps us see
Infinity through the hope of His forgiving mercy.

Does He not offer His firm hand
To loose us from Satan's dark clan,
That we may wed with a holy band,
So as His betrothed, live in an eternal land?

"I have considered my ways and have turned my steps to your statutes. I will hasten and not delay to obey your commands."
(PSALM 119:59–60)

Day Thirty-Two
Intangible Hope

Pray tell me Lord, how I grasp your hope,
An intangible promise beyond my mortal scope?

It has no substance large or small,
Neither height, nor width, short or tall.

It's not within my vision, nor to touch, to smell, or hear.
Yet, you tell me in your Word, it's always so near.

Fear not my precious son and lovely daughter,
For hope comes from my well of living water.

Because hope is found in the flow of Christ's blood,
Washing you, moment by moment, in His love's embracing flood.

"Your word is a lamp to my feet and a light for my path. I have taken an oath and confirmed it, that I will follow your righteous laws."

(PSALM 119:105−106)

Day Thirty-Three
Stay the Course

Stay the course,
Because in life we sometimes declare a spiritual divorce.

Then we return to God on bended knee,
Realizing all along He has been our protecting See.

My lord, help me in my weakness to be firm,
Allow me not to run in fear, so you I spurn.

Help me to give fully over to you
All my weakness in what I fear to do.

"All your commands are trustworthy; help me, for men persecute me without cause. They almost wiped me from the earth, but I have not forsaken your precepts. Preserve my life according to your love, and I will obey the statutes of your mouth."

(PSALMS 119:86-88)

Day Thirty-Four
Hope Leads Home

Sometimes I must say,
My love for you grows day by day.

Your hand alone guides a sure pathway,
Leading to home, an eternal stay.

"Better is one day in your courts than a thousand elsewhere; I would rather be a doorkeeper in the house of my God than dwell in the tents of the wicked."

(PSALM 84:10)

Day Thirty-Five
Perfect Love in Hope

Everyone wants somebody to love.
We're not talking of a pet or turtle dove,

But someone to hold, someone who will be bold,
To be faithful, steadfast, and never be told

You don't love me enough.
I feel what you give is emotional slough,

Drenched, spellbound, enamored. This is what we desire.
God made us to be another's passion of fire.

What we seek will be found at one Man's feet,
Because in His death, Satan suffered defeat.

Only Jesus can offer promise and hope endured,
As He in perfect love gave life only He secured.

"I love the Lord, for he heard my voice; he heard my cry for mercy.
Because he turned his ear to me, I will call on him as long as I live."

(PSALM 116:1–2)

Day Thirty-Six
Simplicity of Hope

Hope can be like a helium-filled balloon.
Try as you might, you'll catch it later than soon.

It seems to bounce from here to there,
Freely dancing around, with nary a care.

Or, could it be, this is not really the case?
Are we not confusing hope with grace?

They come together, don't you see,
Neither is considered by God to be treated lightly.

So if we want God's hope in its entirety,
Bathe in His grace in its pure simplicity.

"Let the sea resound, and everything in it, the world, and all who live in it. Let the rivers clap their hands, let the mountains sing together for joy; let them sing before the Lord, for he comes to judge the earth. He will judge the world in righteousness and the peoples with equity."

(PSALM 98:7–9)

Conclusion

"When I said, 'My foot is slipping,' your love, O Lord, supported me. When anxiety was great within me, your consolation brought joy to my soul."

(PSALM 94:18-19)

www.ingramcontent.com/pod-product-compliance
Lightning Source LLC
Chambersburg PA
CBHW061303040426
42444CB00010B/2488